Memory

Powerful Ways to Naturally Improve Learning, Studying, Reading and Retention with Quick Results!

Robert S. Lee

Contents

The trademarks that are used are without any consent, and the publication of the trademark is without permission or backing by the trademark owner. All trademarks and brands within this book are for clarifying purposes only and are the owned by the owners themselves, not affiliated with this document.

Introduction

Memory allows you to recall important pieces of information throughout the day. It ensures that you are productive and able to manage various tasks. If your memory is poor, you may forget important things and which tasks need to be completed. In today's society where everyone is on the go, stress plays a major role in memory problems. Of course, memory also starts to decline as you get older.

You do not have to settle for a poor memory because there many ways to improve your memory naturally. You can start today and you will notice that your memory starts improving rather quickly. Most of the techniques that you use to improve your memory will also improve your health overall. Just make sure that you are diligent about these techniques to reap the most benefits.

When you have a poor memory, it can affect you in many ways, such as:

- Forgetting where you put something important like your car keys or your glasses
- Getting distracted easily
- Having difficulty remembering conversation details or the details or something that you just read
- Not being able to easily retrieve information when you need it
- Forgetting why you just walked into room
- Forgetting about appointments and meetings that are important
- Forgetting what the names of your acquaintances are

As your memory loss continues, it can cause more problems in your life. When you are doing things like forgetting appointments and meetings or being easily distracted, this can have a negative impact on your career.

As soon as you start to notice memory problems, take the steps necessary to correct them. This guide provides you with all of the information that you need to start improving your memory today. Use the information in this book to improve your life overall and to regain control of your life and your career.

All of the methods in this book are natural and as long as you are using them properly, you are sure to reap the benefits. These natural methods are proven and are used throughout the world to help improve memory, overall health and your ability to learn new things.

In addition to following all of the natural methods in this book to improve your memory, make sure that you are following a healthy lifestyle overall. This will work with your memory-boosting techniques to make them more effective. For example, there are many foods that work to help you to improve your memory and when you add them to a healthy diet that is well-balanced, they will work even better.

You can use these techniques regardless of the reason for your memory difficulties. However, if your memory problems are related to an actual medical problem, make sure that you are also following the treatments that your doctor has prescribed. You can use these techniques with almost all medical treatments to enhance their effectiveness on your memory. Just talk to your doctor first to ensure safety and so that your doctor is aware of the things you are doing at home to boost your energy.

Make sure that you read this book completely so that you get the full benefit. All of these techniques work to boost your memory and you can rest assured that you will get results.

Chapter 1. Foods and Eating Changes to Boost Memory

Your diet plays a major role in your memory and overall brain function. It is important to eat plenty of foods that work to nourish your brain so that your memory is as strong as possible. In addition to the foods you eat, how you eat them also plays a role. Understanding this is the first step in improving your memory so that you are able to get more done and not forget about important events.

Best Memory-Boosting Foods

There are a variety of foods that contain certain nutrients that help to boost your memory. When you eat these foods, you will notice an acute boost in your memory, as well as a long-term improvement in your ability to make memories and recall them in the future. Consider adding the following foods to your diet to ensure that your remember everything that is important:

- **Whole grains:** Whole grains help to provide your brain with energy via glucose. Your brain requires glucose to function optimally for better focus, concentration and memory.

- **Oily fish:** Oily fish are rich in omega-3 fatty acids, a nutrient that works to boost your brain power and prevent the inflammation that may cause issues with your cognitive function. Eating fatty fish two to three days a week will help to ensure that you are getting adequate amounts of this nutrient.

- **Blueberries:** Blueberries are one of the most powerful superfoods because they are full of critical nutrients and antioxidants. When you eat blueberries, you are working toward better cognitive function. In fact, a study shows that blueberries improve your short-term memory and help to protect against short-term memory loss.

- **Tomatoes:** Tomatoes contain a powerful antioxidant referred to as lycopene. This nutrient protects the cells in your brain against free radical damage. Since this type of damage is associated with an increased risk of Alzheimer's disease and other forms of dementia, reducing the damage decreases your risk of such conditions.

- **Pumpkin seeds:** These seeds provide you with a big boost of zinc. Zinc is a mineral that you need to have better thinking skills and memory. A single handful of these seeds is plenty for giving you all of the zinc that you need each day.

- **Broccoli:** This green vegetable is a rich source of vitamin K. This vitamin plays a crucial role in improving brain power and overall cognitive function.

- **Nuts:** Snacking on nuts throughout the day will ensure that you are getting plenty of vitamin E. This vitamin and antioxidant is helpful for preventing cognitive decline so that you can retain your memory as you get older.

- **Dark chocolate:** If you enjoy this sweet treat, you are in luck because it improves the function of the blood vessels in the brain. This ensures that you have optimal memory and cognitive function.

- **Spinach:** Spinach may help to delay or prevent dementia. It also slows down age-related mental decline due to being a rich source of vitamin E and folate.

- **Sunflower seeds:** This type of seed is rich in omega-3 fatty acids, tryptophan and B vitamins, all of which are critical for brain health. Eating sunflower seeds on a regular basis can improve your memory and your mood.

- **Eggs:** Eggs are full of the nutrient choline and this is critical for working in

the brain to ensure adequate memory
formation by working to encourage the
creation of certain neurotransmitters.
This nutrient also plays an important
role in the normal development of the
brain.

Intermittent Fasting for Better Memory

Intermittent fasting is very popular for
promoting weight loss, but it comes with other
positive effects, such as boosting your energy.
This type of fasting involves refraining from
food for a specific amount of time each day,
every day. This type of diet is becoming more
and more popular due to the health benefits.

When it comes to your memory, intermittent
fasting works to preserve learning and memory

function. It further promotes brain health by reducing free radical damage and inflammation, both of which can interfere with your memory and overall cognitive function.

Studies on intermittent fasting show that this type of diet change is believed to promote health benefits, including better memory, by forcing the cells in the body to experience mild stress. This stress helps the cells to better adapt and this results in your cells being better at coping with stress. Scientists think that this may also help the cells to resist disease.

Chapter 2. Using Tea and Coffee for Better Brain Power

Coffee and tea are two of the most common types of beverages and they have many brain-health benefits, including working to boost your memory. If you sip on coffee and tea as you study or work, it can make it easier to recall information and retain new information. The key is knowing the types of coffee and tea to drink and how to best drink them to get the memory-enhancing benefits.

Memory-Boosting Teas

There are a number of teas that can boost your memory and provide other cognitive benefits.

Part of the reason that certain teas are so effective is because they often contain caffeine. However, teas possess other compounds and nutrients that help with memory. Knowing the teas to drink will help you to naturally start boosting your memory while drinking teas that also promote better overall health.

The first two teas that are great for memory and also very common are black tea and green tea. Both work to stop the activity of an enzyme that may increase the risk of Alzheimer's and future memory problems. Green tea goes even further and stops this activity for as long as a week after drinking a single cup. Black tea, while able to also stop the enzyme activity, was only able to do so for about a day. This means that green tea is more powerful and this may be related to the fact that it contains more antioxidants and brain-boosting compounds compared to black tea. However, both teas are proven to help memory so you can choose the one that you prefer most.

There are other teas that you can look into to boost your memory and other aspects of your brain health:

- **Sage tea:** This type of tea helps to improve cognition, mood and mental performance.
- **Saffron tea:** This orange spice may have effectiveness similar to certain medications used to stabilize the mood. It also works to promote a stronger memory.
- **Turmeric tea:** This type of tea works to reduce inflammation, improve memory, influence both dopamine and serotonin and alleviate mood swings and depression.

- **Chamomile tea:** This tea is most commonly used to alleviate anxiety and insomnia. However, it also plays a role in your memory by helping you to get adequate sleep.

- **Lemon balm tea:** This tea is energizing while also helping you to focus. It helps to promote a better memory and level of concentration when you are experiencing stress.

- **Yerba mate tea:** This type of tea may stall dementia and Alzheimer's disease. Other benefits include improving sleep, mood and mental clarity.

- **Masala chai tea:** This is an ayurvedic tea that stabilizes your mood and boosts your memory.

- **Lavender tea:** Lavender has an array of benefits, including lifting your mood,

promoting relaxation and helping you to
recall memories and information.

- **Fennel tea:** This type of tea keeps your glucose levels stable and boosts endorphins and serotonin. These actions help to enhance your memory and prevent mood swings.

- **Ginseng tea:** Ginseng is a very popular tea for memory enhancement. It may also work to stabilize your mood by aiding in serotonin production.

- **Rooibos tea:** This tea is well-known for helping to alleviate stress and anxiety. By relieving these issues, it can help you with your memory.

Enhancing Your Memory with Coffee

Coffee possesses a number of health benefits, especially associated with your brain and memory. When it comes to coffee, it is mostly the caffeine that boosts your memory. A number of studies have been done on how caffeine works to boost memory and most conclude that drinking caffeinated coffee can improve your memory for as long as 24 hours after drinking a cup. This means that you do not have to drink coffee all day to get the benefits. Your morning cup of coffee is often enough to boost your memory for the remainder of the day.

Caffeine benefits your memory in two primary ways. The first is that it makes it harder for you to forget the memories that are already stored.

The second way caffeine helps is by strengthening your memories. This means that they are easier to recall when you need them. In addition to boosting your memory, caffeine has other effects that are beneficial for your brain and cognitive health. These beneficial effects include increasing your attention and making it easier to focus on the task at hand. This works to prevent procrastination and promote greater productivity.

Chapter 3. Boosting Nutrients for a Better Memory

The Western diet is notorious for not providing adequate amounts of certain nutrients that your brain needs for optimal function. This often leads to age-related memory problems that are largely preventable most of the time as long as you are getting the right nutrients. These nutrients are not a cure, but when you have adequate amounts in the body, they naturally support your memory and cognitive function. Even those with conditions like Alzheimer's disease can benefit from getting the right nutrients when it comes to memory. When you are working on getting more

nutrients for brain health, start with focusing
on vitamins and minerals:

- **Vitamin E:** Vitamin E is a critical
  vitamin that doubles as an antioxidant.
  It works to protect the health of your
  brain and ward off brain disorders that
  can affect your memory. You can get this
  vitamin from a supplement or work the
  following foods into your diet: green
  leafy vegetables, sunflower oil, whole
  grains, almonds, corn oil and hazelnuts.
  Some research suggests that this vitamin
  may also help to delay Alzheimer's
  disease progression.

- **Vitamin B12:** Vitamin B12 is a vitamin
  that helps to form the protective
  covering on the nerves in the brain.
  When this covering is compromised, you
  can experience an array of symptoms,
  depending on the exact nerves that are

affected. Memory and cognitive problems are common when you do not get enough vitamin B12. Foods that contain this vitamin include a variety of meats and fortified foods.

- **Vitamin B6:** This B vitamin supports brain health and improves memory retention. Those who regularly get adequate levels of vitamin B6 tend to have better memory over the long-term. You can get more of this vitamin in your diet by eating more tuna, carrots and eggs.

- **Other B vitamins:** The other B vitamins are also very important for the health of your brain. These vitamins help to form epinephrine, dopamine and serotonin, chemicals in your brain that are critical for memory, mood and overall cognitive function. Studies show that those who do not get enough of these nutrients are more likely to experience a decline in memory as they age. Other studies show that low levels of B12, B6 and folic acid are associated with Alzheimer's disease.

- **Magnesium:** Magnesium helps to stop neurotoxins from negatively affecting the brain. This helps to prevent damage that can lead to memory loss and other issues that can occur in the brain. You can get more magnesium in your diet by eating more seeds, whole grains, nuts and dark leafy greens.

- **Vitamin C:** This vitamin is most well-known for its ability to boost your immune system, but its powerful antioxidant properties also help to enhance memory and overall brain health. Vitamin C also works to prevent brain cell damage and age-related memory loss. Eat more citrus fruits and broccoli to get more of this vitamin.

- **Vitamin D:** Vitamin D deficiencies are not uncommon and one of the negative effects of this deficiency is memory loss and problems with cognition. Low vitamin D levels also increase the risk of dementia. You can get vitamin D from the sun and fortified foods.

Other Nutritional Substances for Memory Enhancement

Certain other nutritional supplements may help to promote a better memory. These are nutrients that you can get in foods and they also come in supplement form. Talk to your doctor to determine which form is best for you. For example, if you are on a special diet, you may benefit more from a supplement to ensure the right dose every day. Consider the following nutrients when you are working to improve your memory:

- **DHA:** DHA is a type of omega-3 fatty acid. Research shows that getting enough DHA every day can improve how quickly you are able to recall your short-term memories. This is important for those like students who need to remember recent information for tests and assignments.

- **Antioxidants:** Antioxidants play a critical role in brain health and memory because they fight against the free radicals that can impair memory and cause damage in the brain. You need to get antioxidants on a regular basis so that there is a constant source to fight against the free radicals.

- **Omega-3 fatty acids:** Omega-3 fatty acids are critical for many functions in your body, including brain function and memory enhancement. They also help to reduce cholesterol and inflammation, both of which can contribute to memory problems

- **Acetyl L-carnitine**: This nutrient is an amino acid with the ability to cross the blood brain barrier to nourish the brain for optimal health. It also protects brain cells and acts as a powerful antioxidant.

- **Alpha GPC:** This is a type of choline, a nutrient that is critical for mental focus, recall, attention span and other important brain function.

- **L-carnosine:** This nutrient is a broad-spectrum antioxidant that helps to protect the tissues and cells in the brain. It also defends against age-related mental decline to prevent memory problems as you age.

- **CoQ10:** CoQ10 naturally occurs in the body and it plays a major role in memory and concentration. Research also show that it may help to protect you from Parkinson's disease, types of dementia and age-related memory decline.

- **DMAE:** DMAE supplements help to enhance mood and alertness. It also helps with concentration and mental energy.

- **L-tyrosine:** This is a type of amino acid that is critical for optimal brain function. It works to improve your mood, memory and your response to stress. It also improves overall cognitive performance.

Chapter 4. Improving Gut Health for Better Memory

You already know that what you eat plays a major role in the health of your memory and this is largely due to how your gut utilizes these foods. This means that you need to have a healthy gut to reap the most benefits from the nutrients that you get every day. There is a connection between your brain and your gut as well and when your gut is not healthy, you can experience issues like memory problems, difficulty with focus and concentration and mood issues.

Your body produces a hormone that helps you to feel your best and this is called serotonin. The majority of the serotonin that the body produces is in your digestive tract. Serotonin plays a major role in your ability to remember things and your overall cognitive function. Tryptophan, a type of amino acid, is responsible for the manufacturing of serotonin and you get tryptophan from your diet. Your gut needs to properly digest tryptophan-containing foods to ensure that you have enough to manufacture serotonin. Foods that are rich in tryptophan include:

- Almonds
- Beans
- Chicken
- Fish
- Milk
- Soy-based foods

- Yogurt

- Bananas

- Cheese

- Eggs

- Peanuts

- Turkey

To keep your gut healthy, probiotics are probably the most important factor, but there are certain other nutrients that you want to focus on. These will ensure a healthy gut and they will also make sure that your body is producing enough serotonin to promote optimal memory and overall cognitive health. These nutrients include:

- Certain foods contain serotonin that is completely formed to help boost serotonin levels, including kiwis, plantains, tomatoes, bananas, pineapples, plums and walnuts

- Calcium, vitamin B and magnesium
- Omega-3 fatty acids
- Healthy carbohydrates from whole grains
- Digestive enzymes

In addition to getting the right nutrients, there are certain foods that have a direct role in improving gut health, including:

- **Bananas:** Bananas may reduce inflammation and restore gut bacteria health.
- **Jerusalem artichokes:** This type of artichoke has strong probiotic potential.
- **Cruciferous vegetables:** These vegetables include broccoli, cabbage, kale and cauliflower. These vegetables help to reduce inflammation in the gut.

- **Polenta:** Polenta helps to promote a healthy gut by keeping the digestive tract moving along due to being high in fiber.

- **Beans:** Beans are high in fiber and short-chain fatty acids. These nutrients help to improve micronutrient absorption, strengthen intestine cells and keep your digestive tract moving.

- **Blueberries:** Blueberries enhance your immune system by modifying the microbiota in your gut.

When your gut is healthy, this typically means that you do not often experience digestive issues. If you frequently have the following symptoms, this may indicate that you need to improve the health of your gut:

- Constipation
- Diarrhea
- Nausea

- Gas

- Bloating

Proper Use of Probiotics

Probiotics are likely the easiest way to promote gut health because there are several forms. You know that the health of your gut plays a major role in the health of your memory and probiotics are one of the most important factors in gut health. Knowing how to use probiotics properly ensures that you are reaping the most benefits.

Your gut is home to healthy bacteria that help to ensure healthy digestion and other functions. You want to ensure that this bacteria stays healthy and in balance and this is where probiotics come in. Probiotics are a type of microorganism that is generally a type of bacteria or something like a yeast. They are like the healthy bacteria that already live in your digestive tract.

Probiotics are generally safe as long as you take them as directed. You also want to make sure that you are using a high-quality brand. Talk to your doctor before adding a probiotic supplement just to ensure that you are using it properly. Your doctor can also recommend a brand that you can trust will contain what the label states.

Chapter 5. Exercise and Memory

It is well-established that regular exercise is helpful for promoting memory and better brain health. Exercise improves your ability to think and remember things both indirectly and directly. When you exercise, you are reducing inflammation, decreasing insulin resistance and stimulating growth factor release. Growth factors are responsible for brain cell health and the growth of new blood vessels.

When it comes to indirectly improving your memory, exercise helps to reduce issues that can cause memory loss, such as improving your sleep and mood and reducing anxiety and stress. Without these issues, you are far less likely to experience cognitive impairment.

The media temporal cortex and the prefrontal cortex in the brain are largely responsible for controlling memory and thinking. Research shows that those who exercise regularly tend to have more volume in these two areas of the brain, thus having better memory. If you start exercising regularly today, you can have greater volume in these areas of your brain in as little as six to 12 months. Other memory-boosting benefits of exercise are noticeable with a single vigorous workout.

The key to using exercise to boost memory is knowing how to exercise properly to reap the most benefits. You want to create an exercise plan that works your entire body while focusing on aerobic exercise. Aerobic exercise increases how much oxygen your brain is getting and when your brain is getting more oxygen, it is able to function more efficiently. It also sends more blood to your brain which delivers more sugar and nutrients so that your brain has everything that it requires to ensure proper cognitive function and the ability to recall and retrieve memories with ease.

Creating an Effective Exercise Routine

You want to ensure that you are getting adequate aerobic exercise, but there are three other types of exercise to incorporate into your week. Working four types of exercise into your week sounds like a lot, but it is pretty easy to get all of the exercise that you need. Use this information as a guideline for getting the right amounts of cardiovascular exercise:

- 150 minutes of cardiovascular exercise every week

- 60 minutes of strength training that targets all major muscle groups each week

- 60 minutes of flexibility training every week

- 60 minutes of balance training every week

The most critical type of exercise for improving your memory is aerobic, or cardiovascular, exercise. This is the type of exercise that you want to get the most of because it helps your memory, as well as improves the health of your lungs and heart. There are many aerobic exercises you can do, including:

- Running or jogging

- Swimming

- Cycling

- Hiking

- Doing vigorous yard or house work

- Dancing
- Brisk walking
- Participating in active sports

You can switch between activities to keep things interesting. You can also break your workout up into 10 minute increments to easily fit aerobic exercise in your day.

Strength training is critical for keeping your bones and muscles strong. When you are stronger, you maintain independence and are able to easily take care of everyday tasks. When you are working on creating a strength training plan, there are several options, including:

- Perform resistance training with resistance bands
- Do calisthenics, such as pushups, lunges, sit-ups and squats
- Lift weights

You can do a combination of these exercises to improve your strength. When you are creating your strength training routine, make sure that you strength train every other day so that your muscles have time to relax and repair themselves in between workouts.

Balance training is important for helping you to be more stable on your feet. This is especially important for older adults and those who are disabled due to being at a higher risk for falls. You can work balance exercises in throughout the day whenever you have a few minutes. Just track what you are doing so that you can be sure that you are getting in your 60 minutes a week. Consider the following types of balance exercises to get started:

- Standing on one foot
- Tai chi
- Heel-to-toe walk

If your balance is poor, you can stand next to something that you can quickly grab onto if your balance starts to get shaky. It is important to make sure that you are safe while improving your balance.

Flexibility exercises help to stretch your muscles, but this also helps you to improve your balance. When your muscles are limber and flexible, you have greater range of motion. This allows you to do other exercises, housework and other activities with greater ease. Better flexibility can also help to reduce your pain, especially if it is related to muscle tightness. Good stretching workouts to get started with include:

- Yoga
- Touching your toes
- Pointing your fingers at the ceiling

Just make sure that you are addressing all of your major muscle groups so that you have overall flexibility.

It is important to consider safety when you are exercising to prevent injury. As an added bonus, when you exercise properly, you are improving your memory more because you are reaping the full benefits of exercise. Start by talking to your doctor to ensure that you are healthy enough to perform exercise. In some cases, you may have to modify how you exercise to ensure that you are exercising safely.

When you are exercising, make sure that you are using proper form. This is especially important with strength training because poor form puts you at a significant risk for injury. When you are performing aerobic exercise, know your target heart rate and monitor your heart rate so that you are able to maintain it to reap the most benefits of this type of exercise.

Wear the right shoes and comfortable clothing when you are exercising. When it comes to exercises that involve weights, make sure that you are not using weights that are too heavy for you.

Lastly, when you start exercising, start slow and build up. You want to improve your health over time to prevent injury and reap the most benefits from regular exercise.

Chapter 6. Sleep and Memory

Sleep is restorative and without adequate sleep, your brain does not get the rest that it needs to function optimally. It is important to balance your sleep because too much sleep can also have negative effects on your memory. A nurses' health study conducted at Harvard University concluded that people who sleep approximately seven hours per day maintain their memory better as they get older. This amount of sleep every evening helps you to remember better now and it also prevents age-related mental impairment. To balance your sleep, you want to get no less than seven hours per night and no more than nine hours per night.

Sleep deprivation can lead to conditions like diabetes, high blood pressure and blood vessel narrowing. All of these negatively affect the flow of blood in the brain. When your brain is not getting adequate blood flow, it is not getting the sugar, oxygen and other nutrients that it needs for optimal health. One of the consequences of not getting adequate nutrients is impaired memory and thinking. To show a quick summary of the benefits of adequate sleep, look at the following:

- Not getting enough sleep impairs your ability to efficiently learn and focus.
- For your memories and what you learn to stick, you must get adequate sleep. This ensures that you can recall important information in the future.

Now you know about how much sleep to get each night and why the right amount is so important for your memory. However, not only do you need a certain amount of sleep, but your sleep also has to be high in quality so that your brain is fully rested, refreshed and rejuvenated. Continue reading to learn about what you can do to ensure that you are getting great sleep every night.

Tips to Improve Your Sleep

There are a number of lifestyle changes to make and health habits to break to ensure that you are getting the best sleep possible. This process is referred to as improving your sleep hygiene and as you work toward this, you will ensure that you are getting adequate sleep and that your sleep is high in quality. As long as you are doing these properly and on a daily basis, you can be sure that you will notice sleep improvements in as little as a few days.

Avoid all things that can interfere with your sleep. There are substances like alcohol, nicotine, caffeine and other chemicals that prevent you from getting restful sleep. About six hours before you head to bed, refrain from consuming anything that contains these. Caffeine and nicotine are stimulants so they can prevent you from falling asleep. Alcohol is a depressant, but it can make you toss and turn as you sleep so that your sleep is not restful enough to allow for a fully refreshing sleep.

Create a pre-sleep routine that promotes relaxation. About 30 minutes prior to your bedtime, you want to start preparing your mind and body for sleep. Engage in activities that are relaxing, such as meditating or doing yoga. Avoid activities that are stimulating, such as using your computer or cellphone, watching television, doing vigorous exercise or working. Some people find a warm bath helpful because this causes your body temperature to rise while you are in the bath and then fall quickly after you get out. This rapid temperature change promotes drowsiness so that you are able to fall asleep. Other relaxing activities include reading, deep breathing or simply lying back and reflecting on the positive parts of your day. Just try to avoid thinking about negative things because this can keep you awake.

Make sure that your bedroom is focused on sleep. Your bedroom should be a place of relaxation and sleep. Things that stimulate you like work and homework should never be done in your bedroom. Keep the temperature between 60 degrees Fahrenheit and 75 degrees Fahrenheit because if your room is too hot you will not be able to sleep well. Some people also find that turning a fan on low is soothing and helps to keep them cool enough to sleep. Lastly, ensure that your mattress, bedding and sleeping clothes are comfortable so that you can fully relax in bed.

Create a solid sleeping schedule. People who have a set bedtime and wake time tend to sleep more effectively each night. You should also maintain this sleep schedule on the weekends. Your body will get used to sleeping and waking at certain times, making it easier to fall asleep and sleep through the night. You should avoid variations of more than an hour with this schedule. If for some reason you are unable to follow this schedule for a day, simply get back to your schedule the next evening. Trying to sleep more the next day can actually do more damage to your sleep rhythms.

Avoid napping during the day. There are times when you are tired, but it is important to do things other than napping to restore your energy. When you nap, you can make it to where your body is not tired at your normal bedtime, forcing you to toss and turn and not get enough sleep that night. You can do things like get some exercise or eat an energy-promoting snack to get the energy that you need to get through the rest of the day. If you absolutely must take a nap, it should end at least five hours before your sleep time and it should not exceed 30 minutes.

Watch what you eat and drink before bed. If you drink too much before you go to bed, you will find yourself getting up in the night to use the bathroom, disrupting your sleep. Keep a glass of water at your bedside just in case you get thirsty in the middle of the night. As for food, you want to avoid foods that can cause digestive discomfort, such as spicy foods and foods that are high in carbohydrates. A light snack that contains tryptophan is ideal if

you need a bedtime snack to help yourself sleep
better.

Chapter 7. Herbs for Better Memory

Herbs are one of the most common natural remedies to improve your memory and prevent memory decline. There are a number of herbs that have research showing that they have a positive effect on memory. Just make sure that you are using these herbs exactly as directed to ensure that you reap the most benefits. Explore the variety of herbs that promote memory and choose one that you think will help your memory issues the most.

Ginkgo biloba is one of the most popular herbs for promoting memory. This herb protects your memory and the overall health of your brain due to containing chemicals that possess powerful antioxidants, including terpenoids and flavornoids. These fight free radicals to keep your brain healthy. Studies show that older adults who take this herb do experience memory enhancement. In addition to helping healthy people boost their memory, it also helps to improve thinking and memory in those with vascular dementia and Alzheimer's disease by protecting the nerve cells that contribute to these functions.

Ginseng is another very popular herb for promoting memory. It may be beneficial for improving memory impairment as well. Rat studies show that ginseng extracts help the rats to better navigate mazes because they are able to better remember the routes that did not help them to find the exit. It promotes memory enhancement by activating the neurotransmitter activities responsible for your memory. Ginseng also helps to increase your energy which helps to alleviate memory impairment that is associated with fatigue and stress. The energy increase is gentle and it does not cause the jitteriness that you often experience with caffeine.

Sage has a variety of active ingredients that increase the chemicals that are responsible for causing message transmission in the brain. A study of 44 people proved that sage has a positive effect on memory. In this study, some people took a placebo and others took sage. Those who took the actual sage had a better performance on word recall testing. Other experiments show that sage is also beneficial for improving memory in those who have Alzheimer's disease because it increases the brain chemicals that are reduced in those who have this disease.

Rosemary is a common cooking herb, but also has powerful memory improvement properties.

This herb has the ability to neutralize the free radicals that can cause damage that is responsible for memory loss. This is thanks to rosemary containing healthy doses of antioxidants. This herb has a twofold effect because it not only helps to improve memory, but it can reduce certain things that can make your memory worse. These memory-reducing factors that rosemary is helpful for includes poor concentration, intense stress and a poor level of focus. Improvements in these factors will remove the roadblocks that can cause you to forget things because your mind is essentially elsewhere.

Rhodiola rosea has been used for centuries for memory issues and it is known as one of the best herbal options for memory enhancement. It works to improve memory and increase your ability to focus so that you can better recall and retrieve information. It also helps to alleviate depression, a condition that can contribute to memory problems. The adaptogenic properties of this herb are mildly stimulating and this helps to improve concentration and focus too. One study shows that those who take this herb on a regular basis experience improved memorization abilities that improve more with time.

Green tea extract is an extract that comes from the herbs responsible for green tea. It has powerful antioxidant properties and it helps to prevent damage that may contribute to memory issues. In fact, animal research proves that this extract is helpful in preventing age-related decline in the hippocampus and it improves spatial learning abilities. The use of this herb goes back centuries as a mild stimulant and memory enhancer. In fact, there are studies that back up the claims that green tea extract works to enhance memory, learning, concentration and focus, as well as alleviate certain factors that can contribute to poor memory, such as stress and fatigue.

Gotu kola is most popular for its stimulant effects, but it also helps to improve brain function and enhance the memory. These benefits are partly due to the stimulant properties, but it also contains other natural chemicals that contribute to this. This herb is commonly used as an anti-aging herb in ayurvedic and Traditional Chinese Medicine. Health practitioners in this fields recommend gotu kola as a remedy to rejuvenate both the mind and body to prevent the effects of aging. It benefits brain health in another way by increasing circulation to the brain. Other benefits include better intelligence, concentration and attention span.

Bacopa is an herb that you do not hear about too often because it is one of the most powerful memory-enhancing herbs available. Many studies have been done on this herb to determine its ability to boost mental function and memory. The majority of the studies have concluded that those who take this herb on a regular basis find that they have better memory and increased mental health. This herb has been used for centuries in ayurvedic medicine to enhance concentration, memory and learning. It also helps to promote a higher level of cognitive processing.

Periwinkle is a popular plant for better memory because the leaves and seeds of the plant contain a vinpocetine precursor called vincamine. This chemical helps to ensure adequate circulation to the brain so that it gets the oxygen and nutrients that it requires for optimal function. It also encourages better use of oxygen by the brain to naturally enhance your memory.

Huperzia is a popular Chinese herb that works as an acetylcholinesterase inhibitor. This works to improve memory by increasing the brain's cholinergic activity. It also helps to protect the nerves in the brain from glutamate-related damage by working as an NMDA receptor antagonist. Human trials studying the efficacy of this herb conclude that this herb works to improve memory and cognitive function, as well as protect against neurodegeneration.

Ashwagandha works like a happy herb because it improves mood and has aphrodisiac effects. It also helps to improve cognitive function to enhance your memory. In studies, the root of this herb is becoming promising as a potential treatment for Alzheimer's disease.

The research shows that it may be able to breakdown the plaques that are associated with this disease to alleviate the symptoms, including memory impairment.

Safe and Proper Use of Herbs

While herbs are all natural and generally safer than medications, it is important to remember that natural does not automatically mean safe. Since herbal supplements are not regulated, there is no proof that it contains what it claims. Because of this, make sure that you are using a trusted brand so that you are getting the right herb at the right dose so that you get the benefits from taking the supplement.

When you are reading the label on a supplement bottle, look at the following so that you know exactly what you are taking:

- The name of the herb on the front of the label
- The contact information and name of the distributor or manufacturer
- Amount, serving size and active ingredient
- Complete list of ingredients

If you need help reading the label or understanding the information, talk to your pharmacist or doctor. They will ensure that you take the herb properly for optimal safety and maximum benefits.

Now that you understand what to be on the lookout for, use the following tips to ensure optimal safety and efficacy when you are using herbs to boost your memory:

- Follow the administration instructions on the bottle exactly. Never take more than is recommended.
- Only use supplements manufactured in the United States to ensure optimal safety.
- Make note of what you are taking, the dose, how often and how much it is helping you.
- Talk to your doctor before taking a supplement to ensure that it does not interact with anything else that you take.

Before you use an herb, make sure that your pharmacist or doctor knows if you take any of the following:

- Blood clotting disorders

- Diabetes

- Epilepsy

- Heart disease

- Immune system disorders

- Parkinson's disease

- History of stroke

- Cancer

- Enlarged prostate gland

- Glaucoma

- High blood pressure

- Thyroid issues

- Kidney or liver problems

If you have these conditions, there are still
herbs that you can take safely. However, the
dose may need to be adjusted. Your doctor may
also recommend an alternate herb that has the
same actions that will be safer for you.

When it comes to herbs, it is important to remember that they are largely safe, but you just need to take a few precautions before you start taking them to ensure optimal safety. If you follow the information here, you will be able to choose the memory-boosting herbs that will work the best for you and be safe for you.

Chapter 8. Aromatherapy for Memory

It is well-known that certain scents trigger memories from your past. For example, if you smell your grandmother's perfume, it makes you think about her. Aromatherapy is an ancient form of medicine that uses essential oils and other types of aromatic compounds to improve well-being. There are several scents that can trigger memory to help you remember important things and events from your past.

Aromatherapy is thought to work in two ways. The first way is to influence the way the brain remember things. The limbic system in the brain takes scents and essentially translates them into thoughts. So, when you smell something that you smelled in the past, you can remember where the smell came from. The second way is that the scents have a pharmacological effect. When you smell essential oils, they work like medications, but without the risk of negative side effects.

The first thing you need to do to use aromatherapy is know which essential oils work to promote better memory. There are several scents to choose from, allowing you to choose one that you really like. There are also mixtures that you can use to enhance your memory. The following individual oils are common memory boosters:

- **Lavender:** This oil is very common for calmness, but it can help to promote memory by calming you enough so that you are able to concentrate. When you are able to concentrate and focus, it is easier to remember thing.

- **Rosemary:** Rosemary oils promote better proscriptive memory. This helps you with things like remembering to schedule appointments, pick up your mail or catch a show on television.

- **Basil:** Basil reduces fatigue-induced distraction and poor memory. If you are studying and you need to remember the information that you are learning.

- **Peppermint:** Peppermint is uplifting and this characteristic helps to promote memory. It helps you to focus your senses, it wakes up your mind and improves overall memory.

- **Cyprus:** This oil is subtler than many of the others, but it still has a powerful ability to improve memory and concentration.

- **Sage:** Sage has a stimulant effect that is able to wake you up so that you can focus and remember things. This oil is ideal in the morning because it stimulates you and helps you to get started with your day without providing too much energy.

- **Ginger root:** This oil helps to calm your thoughts so that you are better able to focus and concentrate. When you can calm your thoughts, racing thoughts will not interfere with your memory.

- **Juniper oil:** This essential oil helps to support your mind. Using this oil when you need to remember something will help to improve your recall speed so that you can quickly retrieve the information that you need.

- **Lemon:** Lemon oil is energizing. It is ideal if you have memory issues associated with feeling fatigued or when you are feeling down. It will uplift you so that these issues are not impairing your memory.

In addition to the single oils, there are various pairings that you can use to enhance your memory. These combinations improve your memory and they also help with things like focus, concentration and alertness. Consider the following essential oil pairings:

- **Blend one:** Create this blend by mixing two drops of lemon oil and three drops of rosemary oil.
- **Blend two:** Create this blend by mixing one drop of basil oil, two drops of cypress oil and two drops of rosemary oil.

- **Blend three:** Create this blend by mixing three drops of lemon oil and two drops of hyssop oil.

- **Blend four:** Create this blend by mixing one drop of peppermint oil and four drops of cypress oil.

- **Blend five:** Create this blend by mixing three drops of lemon oil and two drops of peppermint oil.

Safe and Proper Use of Aromatherapy

To reap the most benefits from aromatherapy, you must use it properly. The first thing you want to ensure is safe use and this involves mixing the oils properly. There are two types of oils that you need when you use aromatherapy:

- **Carrier oils:** This type of oil allows you to safely dilute essential oils so that when you apply them to the skin, there is no irritation.

- **Essential oils:** These are the main oils that you use when you practice aromatherapy. Essential oils are plant products created via distillation and steam expression.

You may need a carrier oil for all forms of aromatherapy, depending on the oil, but carrier oils are almost always necessary when you are using essential oils topically. The general mixture is one teaspoon of carrier oil mixed in with three drops of the memory-boosting essential oil you choose. To ensure the right mixture for the exact oil you are using, read the label on the oil just to ensure that it does not need further dilution because some oils do. Use the following as carrier oils:

- Grapeseed oil

- Apricot kernel oil

- Sweet almond oil

- Avocado oil

- Jojoba oil

Always use organic and cold-pressed carrier oils for the best results. To prevent these oils from spoiling prematurely, always keep them refrigerated.

If you are not using aromatherapy topically, there are a few other options you can consider. These are inhalation methods that are proven to work:

- **Steam:** Boil water and add a few drops of your memory-enhancing essential oil to spread the scent throughout several rooms of your home.

- **Spray:** Fill a spray bottle with water, add a few drops of essential oil and shake it well. You can spray this on things like furniture to have the scent close to you.

- **Diffuser:** Diffusers are one of the easiest ways to use essential oils and they ensure that the scent spreads throughout a room. You will place the oils on the oil tray and then light a small candle below it to heat the scent so that it diffuses.

- **Dry evaporation:** This is a good technique when you want to take a memory-boosting essential oil on the go. Put a few drops of oil on a clean cotton ball and carry this around with you in your wallet or purse so that you can smell the scent when you need it.

Chapter 9. Brain Games for Better Memory

Did you know that your ability to easily remember things starts to decline as early as your late 20s? This means that you need to start exercising your brain at a young age to stay sharp and prevent future problems with your memory. Brain games are an excellent way to exercise your brain and ensure it is functioning optimally. These games are fun and easy to work into your daily schedule too.

There are a variety of brain games online and for major video games consoles. However, you can also use things like Sudoku, crossword puzzles, word find puzzles and other types of puzzle books. You can also put together real puzzles, play checkers or chess or engage in other games that require you to develop a strategy. What is important is that your mind feels challenged as you are playing the game. Other games you can use to improve your memory include:

- **Tricky cups:** In this came, a ball is placed under one cup and there are two cups that have nothing under them. Someone shuffles the cups around and you have to keep watch on the cup with the ball so that once the shuffling stops, you can identify the right cup.
- **Concentration:** Have someone lie 10 playing cards face up so that you have a chance to see where they are. Have them flip the cards so that you cannot see the faces and then ask you to identify a card. You have to use your memory to

remember where that card is. You play the game until all of the cards are face up again.

- **Spot the difference:** There are activity books that have two pictures next to each other. You have to examine the pictures and find the differences between them.

- **Board games:** Many board games make you use your memory to solve problems, such as Clue. In the case of Clue, you have to keep track of the characters, rooms and weapons so that you can make the right guess combination as to who is guilty.

- **Rubik's Cube:** The Rubik's Cube is probably one of the most popular memory games because this cube has been around for decades. You have to get all of the side to have a single matching

color to master this game. This means
that you have to remember the twists
and turns that you have done in the past
so that you do not undo your progress.

Enhance Your Memory by Learning New Things

If you prefer reading and learning over playing games, you are in luck because if you are frequently working to learn new things, this too helps to improve your memory. Constantly learning new things helps to boost your cognitive abilities to improve your memory. Those who read on a daily basis are less likely to experience memory problems in the future. When you read, you are learning new words and exploring new worlds. If you read mystery books, you are constantly storing thoughts to try and solve the mystery before finishing the book.

Chapter 10. Quick and Easy Memory Prompts

Memory prompts help you to take the information that you have memorized and be able to utilize it. These essentially work to jog your memory so that you can quickly retrieve important information when you need it. For example, you can use memory prompts to remember information for tests or for your work tasks.

You can jog your memory in a number of ways, depending on what works best for you. Even if your memory is poor, you likely are retaining the information. The problem occurs when you need to retrieve and use the information. These memory prompts help to prevent this problem so that you can easily access your memories and other information.

When you are working on a task, give your memory's full attention to the task. When you are multi-tasking, it is a lot harder to keep your thoughts and the information you are utilizing in order. You should also focus on a single medium. For example, if you are studying, stick to a book and a notebook or your computer, but do not use both because this can distract your memory.

Retracing your steps is one of the most common ways to prompt your memory. This is a good way to find something when you do not remember where you put it. For example, you know you had your keys when you got home from work, but now you cannot find them. Go back to your vehicle and re-enter your home exactly as you did when you got home the first time.

Talk it out or write it down. If you cannot remember something, talk it out to jog your memory. You can also write things down to help trigger the information that you need. You can also do a combination of both of these. If you are trying to remember information for studying purposes, using a combination of talking and writing is usually the most effective.

Start using pictures to jog your memory. Everyone has a cellphone with a camera on it these days and you can use this to your advantage. One ideal use of pictures is to be able to remember the names and faces of your acquaintances. Snap their picture and name the picture with the person's first and last name. If you ever cannot recall someone's name, just discreetly look in your phone to job your memory.

Try taking a nap. In some cases, difficulty remembering something is related to you being tired. If you take a quick 30 minute nap this refreshes you and rejuvenates your brain function. This is ideal for those who are struggling to get through major tasks, such as creating a presentation for work or studying. In fact, studies have been done on how sleep can improve memory and results show that when you sleep, it actually increases your motor skills and improves your memory.

Meditation is a way to clear your head so that you can push out everything that is causing you to feel overwhelmed. This is a good way to clear your mind so that you can concentrate on what you are trying to remember. You can mediate any time that you need to remember something important. If you meditate on a regular basis, this can help to improve your memory over the long-term. Consider meditating for 10 to 15 minutes each day. This is enough to help balance your mind and body so that everything is working in harmony. It also gives you a chance each day to clear your mind of anything that is congesting it and making it hard to remember things.

Chapter 11. Using Mnemonics for Easy Memory Recall

Mnemonics help you to remember things by turning important information into something that is fun and catchy. Mnemonics are especially helpful if you are in school and you need to remember groups of information, such as the order of operations in a math class. Using mnemonics allows you to commit the information to memory so that when you need to retrieve the information in the future, you can use the mnemonic to trigger your memory. There are multiple mnemonic types that you can choose from, depending on your personal preferences, including:

- **Music mnemonics:** Turn the information that you need to remember into a song. When you need to recall the information, sing the song to yourself to trigger the memory.

- **Name mnemonics:** These work to create a name where the first letter stands for one thing that you need to remember. For example, if you needed to remember the fruits bananas, apples and tangerines, you would use the mnemonic "BAT."

- **Rhyme mnemonics:** These work to help you remember by creating a rhyme. You can recite the rhymes to help you remember the information.

- **Note card mnemonics:** This type involves creating a series of note cards that you will review several times per day. This works to help you memorize the information necessary.

- **Image mnemonics:** Use this type of mnemonic to remember information using images. For example, if you need to remember the different types of depressant drugs, draw a bat. The bat will stand for **B**arbiturates, **A**lcohol and **T**ranquilizers.

- **Connection mnemonic:** Some people find it easier to remember things when they connect the information to something that they are already familiar with.

Try out the different types of mnemonics and see which types work best for you. In many cases, people choose a different mnemonic based on the subject since different ones work better for different things. For example, note card mnemonics tend to work very well for

science and history, while music mnemonics
tend to work very well for math.

You can also use this memory booster for other
areas of your life, such as your career. If you
have a big presentation coming up at work, use
mnemonics to help you to memorize and recall
the important points that you need to touch on.
If you use the note card type, you can always
bring the note cards with you for a little extra
reassurance.

Conclusion

Now that you have reached the end of this guide, you have all of the tools that you need to start enhancing your memory today. Start by choosing one or two methods so that you can perfect them before adding more. This allows you to transition into a memory-friendly lifestyle so that you do not feel overwhelmed with multiple lifestyle changes.

When you start using these techniques, you will notice your memory improving, but you will also notice improvements in other areas of your life, such as your ability to learn new things and your overall health.

People of all ages can use these techniques to improve their memory. Whether you are 19 years old and you are finding it hard to keep up with your college coursework because of your memory, or your memory is getting a little worse with age, these techniques will work for you.

When you are implementing the various memory-boosting techniques in this book, make sure that you are using them properly. For example, you want to ensure the right dosage of herbs and you want to make the teas properly to reap the most benefits. This is all very easy to do so do not worry about any of the techniques being time-consuming or overwhelming.

Now it is time to get started and start enjoying your life with a much stronger memory.

9 781951 083717